RELATIONSHIP GOALS
STUDY GUIDE

RELATIONSHIP
GOALS

How to Win at
DATING, MARRIAGE,
and SEX

STUDY GUIDE

MICHAEL TODD

with Eric Stanford

WATERBROOK

RELATIONSHIP GOALS STUDY GUIDE

All Scripture quotations are taken from the Holy Bible, New Living
Translation, copyright © 1996, 2004, 2007, 2013, 2015 by Tyndale House
Foundation. Used by permission of Tyndale House Publishers Inc., Carol
Stream, Illinois 60188. All rights reserved.

Details in some anecdotes and stories have been changed to protect the
identities of the persons involved.

This work is based on and directly quotes from *Relationship Goals* by Michael
Todd, first published in hardcover by WaterBrook, an imprint of Random
House, a division of Penguin Random House LLC, New York, in 2020.
Relationship Goals copyright © 2020 by Michael Todd.

Trade Paperback ISBN 978-0-593-19260-3
eBook ISBN 978-0-593-19261-0

Copyright © 2020 by Michael Todd

Published in the United States by WaterBrook, an imprint of Random House,
a division of Penguin Random House LLC.

WATERBROOK® and its deer colophon are registered trademarks of Penguin
Random House LLC.

Printed in the United States of America
2020—First Edition

10 9 8 7 6 5 4 3 2 1

SPECIAL SALES
Most WaterBrook books are available at special quantity discounts when
purchased in bulk by corporations, organizations, and special-interest groups.
Custom imprinting or excerpting can also be done to fit special needs. For
information, please email specialmarketscms@penguinrandomhouse.com.

CONTENTS

INTRODUCTION

A *goal* is the result or achievement toward which effort is directed. Take away the goal, and what good is the effort? Imagine an archer with a bow and arrow. If he doesn't have a bull's-eye target, he can aim and shoot if he wants, but the arrow is not going to hit anything purposeful. So, what's the point?

Many of us don't have our aim directed when it comes to relationships. We take whatever comes. We do whatever's comfortable. But we don't really know where we're going or why.

Don't believe me? Have you ever known a girl who dated pretty much any guy who happened to show an interest in her, without ever stopping to think about the kind of guy who would really be right for her? Or a couple who have dated for a long time and have gotten so comfortable with it that they aren't making any move toward marriage? Or a married couple who have let their former passion turn into a business partnership for child rearing and home maintenance?

And it's not just romantic relationships. How about a parent who doesn't have any plans for how to stay close to his kids as they turn into adults and leave the home? Or somebody who moved into the neighborhood a year ago and still hasn't made a single move to get to know her neighbors?

Maybe you're the kind of person who somehow has never gotten around to making conscious relationship goals and has just fallen into the relationship ruts. But more than likely you've got some kind of goals, targets, or markers of success in mind when it comes to relationships. That's better. Still, even if you do have targets, I want you to be open minded about whether these are the *right* targets. You might need to reexamine them. Because, see, it's possible to have a target for your arrow that's the *wrong* target.

Let's say you're single and ready to mingle and you've made a list of things you want in a significant other. One could be "He's got to be at least this tall and make this much money" or "She's got to have a cute face and a tiny waist." This shows that most of our lists tend to be a little (or a lot) superficial and might reflect not what we actually need in a partner but more of just what we want at the time.

Or let's say you want to make more friends. Whom are you interested in knowing better? Is it just because they're good looking, have money, or have surface similarities with you? What about what's on the inside of them?

It's good to take aim at relationship goals. That's a whole lot better than just passively letting society or the media or our family experience teach us how to do relationships. But we also have to make sure we have the right goals, ones that will contribute to the life we ought to be leading.

God will help us find the right target for our relational arrows. And it will be better than what we could find anywhere else.

Culture's views on relationship are a moving target. Culture says marriage looks like this in one decade, then like that in another decade. The term *dating* used to imply physically going out somewhere. But now we have "Netflix and chill," and you don't have to be committed to anybody to cross the line into private areas.

> *You can take aim at new relationship goals to help fulfill your purposes in life and keep you in line with God's eternal truths.*

God wants every single one of us to have successful relationships, but we have to have a goal that is stable enough for us to aim at. So, let me point out to you that the only thing that is unchangeable, unwavering, and immovable is the Word of God. Isaiah 40:8 tells us, "The grass withers and the flowers fade, but the word of our God stands forever." So, I dare you—no, I double-dog dare you—to let the standard of your relationships be God's Word, even if it's just for the time it takes you to go through these five sessions. Let's just see what would happen in our hearts, minds, and lives if we would follow the stable, biblical model of relationships instead of following our own feelings or other people's examples.

In your Relationship Goals group, you can take aim at new relationship goals that will help you fulfill your purposes in life and keep you in line with God's eternal truths.

I don't care how old you are, how many relationships you've had, or what your current relationship status is— you *can* do relationships differently. You just need the right goals, ones that will enable you to get a W.

—Michael Todd

HOW TO USE THIS GUIDE

This study guide works in a lot of different situations, including in small groups, in book discussion groups made up of either single or married people (or both combined), or by a dating or married couple who want to grow closer. However you choose to use this study guide, I hope that you will maximize your experience by using it alongside the book *Relationship Goals*.

If you're studying *Relationship Goals* in an established group, you probably already have a clear sense of how your meetings should be organized and conducted to fit your context. But if you want a little more direction, here are some suggestions to get you started.

THE GROUP EXPERIENCE

To encourage conversation in your Relationship Goals group, try to keep the group size to no more than a dozen people. Meet in a place where you can sit comfortably to discuss the questions. There's enough material for about an hour of meeting time, though you can shrink it or stretch it if you need to, depending on how your group manages the discussion time.

This whole journey is about progression, not perfection. It's important that you have a place to share honestly. So, more than anything, make sure that you're in a group of people you trust. God doesn't bless who you pretend to be. He blesses who you really are.

THE SESSION FORMAT

The sessions are designed to follow a simple format. You'll find an introduction you can read, opening and closing prayers, and a starter question that will help to get the conversation moving. Then you've got three steps:

Step 1: Personal Need—a simple activity or some questions that will help you identify the personal relevance of the topic for you, individually.

Step 2: Group Discussion—a menu of discussion questions designed to help the group understand and apply truths from the book *Relationship Goals,* supplemented with Bible studies that will help you dig into relevant passages.

Step 3: Action Step—your turn to decide what kind of relationship goals you are going to aim for in response to what you've learned in the session.

THE GROUP LEADER

One person should serve as the facilitator of the group sessions. This isn't junior high, and there's no need for anyone to lecture or dominate the group. But someone should take responsibility for keeping the discussion rolling.

Even if someone has had more experience in relationships, I encourage everyone to value everyone else's experience. The leader of the group should see this as an opportunity for service that can be done only with humility and compassion. You don't have to be a relationship expert; you are just helping to facilitate the conversation.

RELATIONSHIPS

This study is all about relationships, right? So, make these sessions an opportunity for building relationships among the group members. Spend time getting to know one another, encouraging and praying for one another. You might want to have your discussion over a meal or serve snacks. By the authority invested in me as a pastor and the author of *Relationship Goals*, I hereby give you permission to make your group fun!

READING SCHEDULE FOR RELATIONSHIP GOALS

If you haven't already read the book *Relationship Goals,* do so as you work your way through these sessions.

- Chapter 1: Read before session 1.
- Chapters 2 and 3: Read before session 2.
- Chapters 4 and 5: Read before session 3.
- Chapters 6 and 7: Read before session 4.
- Chapters 8, 9, and the conclusion: Read before session 5.

SOME SPECIAL ADVICE:
BE HOT!

So many people who are looking for a relationship are trying to find a girl or a guy who is *hot*. And they try to look as *hot* as possible themselves so they can get attention. "Bro, she's smokin' hot!"

For the purposes of this discussion group, let me suggest that you forget how you look or how smooth you act and try to be HOT—Humble, Open, and Transparent.

Your group is going to be talking about relationships. Singleness. Dating. Sex. Marriage. Divorce. It's going to get personal *fast*. It might get pretty hot in the room! And so, you might be tempted to hold back on your own personal story or what you're thinking and feeling or the mistakes you've made. That's your right, if that's what you want to do. But once again I've got a dare for you: be vulnerable and share openly with your group past the point where it feels comfortable to you, because that's where you're going to expose parts of your heart that need healing. You can't walk in freedom until you walk in truth (John 8:32).

Or here's another way to look at it: We all want to become more in our relationships. But before we can become, we have to be. *Be* is the beginning of *be-come*. We have to deal with where we really are first. Positive transformation comes afterward.

To make all this work, your group needs to agree to be a safe place for everybody to be HOT. Got me? You don't judge. You don't tease. You don't gossip. If somebody wants to keep something confidential within the group, all he has to do is say so—and it's done. This kind of trust will make it possible for your group not just to discuss some ideas but also to minister to one another. And isn't that what you want?

> *Be vulnerable and share openly with your group, because that's where you're going to expose parts of your heart that need healing.*

If you're hurting on the inside because of issues with relationships, the Enemy wants you to keep the problems hidden so they continue to ooze like a fresh wound. He wants you listening to his accusations, lies, and discouragement, not taking in words of truth or hope. But Revelation 12:11 tells how the brothers and sisters foil the Enemy's plans.

> They have defeated him by the blood of the Lamb
> and by their testimony.

Did you catch that? "By their testimony." We can't defeat the Enemy without God's grace in Christ (the Lamb), but something else that's crucial is our own testimony—our story of how we've gone wrong, our thankfulness for how Jesus stepped in, our witness to how God is restoring us and moving us toward our purpose. As these stories are shared in a group, we bring the healing truth to one another.

All I did was write the *Relationship Goals* book. *You* are the minister in your Relationship Goals group. So be HOT about your problems and your progress. And let others be HOT too.

RELATIONSHIP GOALS
PURPOSE

Based on chapter 1 of *Relationship Goals:* "Taking Aim."

Session Aim: To recognize the need to have targets in our key relationships, aligning our purposes in these relationships with God's amazing purposes for us.

#RelationshipGoals has been a trending topic worldwide for years now. Search for this hashtag on social media, and you'll find celebrity couples posing at exclusive clubs, stills from romantic movies at the point where the boy gets the girl, cute couples kissing on a beach or cuddled up in bed, a boyfriend-girlfriend pair holding balloons in the park and giving the impression that their relationship has never been anything but pure happiness. And when people re-post these pictures with the hashtag, what are they saying? They're saying, "I want a relationship like that!" Kim and Kanye, Jay and Bey, Prince William and Kate, Will and Jada, some unidentified couple who look really good in a picture that happened to go viral—we can easily become obsessed with their seemingly perfect images and make them our idols and ideals.

Okay, maybe you've never noticed the #Relationship-Goals tag online, much less posted anything with it. But if I were to ask you to think about the relationship you want, would an idealized picture flash into your mind? Maybe it's you with a tall, handsome pro athlete who takes you on shopping sprees. Or maybe it's you beside a girl who's hood like Cardi B but has a sweet side like Carrie Underwood. Is he an amazing listener with a classic swag like George Clooney and a job that pays both his bills and yours? Can she cook like your mama and get just as hype as you do when your team scores?

> *The Bible, in fact, is the greatest source for relationship wisdom, and it's time we started applying it to relationships as they really exist.*

Now, if you just asked *What's wrong with that?* in your head, allow me to submit to you that maybe there's more to relationship than what pop culture has taught us or our own imaginings have dreamed up. Maybe our society sells an illusion of intimate relationship that's more like a mirage—the closer you get to it, the more you realize it's not real at all. Maybe the things we tend to celebrate are built on unstable foundations and are bound to eventually fall.

We live in a world that has more and more relationships and less and less love, more and more sex and less and less intimacy. I wrote *Relationship Goals* because I want others to minimize the pain from bad relationships and start to benefit from the rewards of good ones. Relationship Goals groups are for people who want to talk through these issues with others. Together you can help each other learn how to win in relationships. I'm glad you're in!

Opening Prayer

Holy Spirit, we invite You to come into this group and make it Your own . . . right now! Teach us truths we need to know. Soften our hearts to receive the truth. Begin healing our hurts. Help us to treat one another with respect and help each other move into a life of more holiness, more meaning, and more happiness.

God, whatever we've been through in our relational lives in the past, help us to trust that You have good things ahead for us.

In Jesus's name, amen.

STARTER QUESTION

What made you want to be a part of this Relationship Goals group? What are you hoping to get out of it?

STEP 1: PERSONAL NEED

What's your relationship personality? To start thinking of what you're like as a relater, check out the statements below. Keeping in mind all your important relationships (family, friendship, romantic, professional, and so on), circle the number from 1 to 5 that best describes you.

I'm slow to form relationships.	1 2 3 4 5	I'm quick to form relationships.
I think carefully about the relationships I form.	1 2 3 4 5	I tend to go with my gut in choosing relationships.
My relationships tend to last a long time.	1 2 3 4 5	I tend to go through relationships quickly and move on.
I typically think of relationships as a possible source of hurt or risk.	1 2 3 4 5	I typically think of relationships as a source of happiness and fun.
I have just a few relationships that mean a lot to me.	1 2 3 4 5	I love having lots of relationships.

This is not a right or wrong, better or worse quiz. This is an exercise for you to evaluate how you relate to others and probably some things you never stop to think about.

Based on this nonscientific quiz, and other ways you've gotten to know yourself, how would you summarize your relationship personality—how you generally feel about relationships and go about pursuing them?

STEP 2: GROUP DISCUSSION

1. What was the last post you saw with the hashtag #RelationshipGoals? What does this post say about the culture that surrounds us?

2. Name up to three other misleading images of the "perfect" relationship that you have seen in the media lately—whether in a movie, on a billboard, on social media, or elsewhere. Do you believe the images we see of "perfect" relationships are dangerous, neutral, or helpful in our own relationships and friendships? Why?

3. What rules of romantic relationships did you hear growing up? In what ways were you taught or shown how to follow them?

4. Michael says, "It's no secret that the church hasn't done a great job at confronting real-life issues, so many of us didn't have much choice but to allow movies, TV shows, each big cousin who had a new girlfriend every Thanksgiving, and the slew of insta-famous people who take great filtered photos to become our relationship gurus." In what ways did television, movies, or social media shape your view of relationships while you were growing up?

5. What examples of healthy relationships—whether parent/child, husband/wife, or friendships—did you have around you as you grew up? How do you think they influenced your view of relationships today?

6. In what ways have the church and Jesus followers influenced your view of relationships?

7. In general, are you the kind of person who likes to set goals or the kind of person who likes to wing it? What about in relationships, specifically?

8. Describe a time when having a clear relationship goal helped you achieve what you wanted. Or describe a time when not having a clear relationship goal led to trouble.

{ *We live in a world that has more and more relationships and less and less love, more and more sex and less and less intimacy.* }

9. If someone were to look at your relationships today—in business, school, romance, friendship, or family—what would that person say is your primary goal? Is that what you want it to be? Why or why not?

10. In which of your relationships are you feeling the lack of a goal the most? Why?

11. Michael introduces the idea that our relationship goals are supposed to be in alignment with our major life purposes and the dreams God has planted in us. As you see it, what is the connection between relationships and purpose?

12. Ephesians 2:1–10 beautifully pictures God's mercy to us, taking us from spiritual death to spiritual

life, from enslavement to evil to an invitation to
do good things.

Once you were dead because of your disobe-
dience and your many sins. You used to live
in sin, just like the rest of the world, obeying
the devil—the commander of the powers in
the unseen world. He is the spirit at work in
the hearts of those who refuse to obey God.
All of us used to live that way, following the
passionate desires and inclinations of our sin-
ful nature. By our very nature we were sub-
ject to God's anger, just like everyone else.

But God is so rich in mercy, and he loved
us so much, that even though we were dead
because of our sins, he gave us life when he
raised Christ from the dead. (It is only by
God's grace that you have been saved!) For
he raised us from the dead along with Christ
and seated us with him in the heavenly realms
because we are united with Christ Jesus. So
God can point to us in all future ages as examples of the incredible wealth of his grace
and kindness toward us, as shown in all he
has done for us who are united with Christ
Jesus.

God saved you by his grace when you be-
lieved. And you can't take credit for this; it is
a gift from God. Salvation is not a reward for

the good things we have done, so none of us
can boast about it. For we are God's masterpiece. He has created us anew in Christ Jesus,
so we can do the good things he planned for
us long ago.

a. Do you consider yourself to be saved? If so,
    tell the group about your salvation experi-
    ence. If not, it's okay—you belong here even
    before you believe.

b. What are some of the most obvious ways
    God has shown His love to you and changed
    your life since your salvation?

c. What do you think it means that "we are
    God's masterpiece"?

d. Where are you in understanding and pursuing God's purposes for you—the "good things" He planned for you long ago?

13. Michael points out that culture offers us an unstable picture of relationships. In contrast, the Word of God is unchangeable, unwavering, and immovable. How has the Bible influenced your vision for the relationships in your life?

14. "Progression, not perfection" is Michael's mantra for relationship goals. Is that encouraging to you? If so, why?

15. What does getting a win in relationships mean to you?

> *Having a goal without aim is senseless, but having a goal without God is pointless.*

STEP 3: ACTION STEP

In chapter 1, Michael says there's no pressure to get everything right with our relationship goals all at once—but there *is* pressure to get started. So, let's do that. Write down one to three relationship goals for yourself as you know them at this point. In the course of this study, you'll add to and refine your goals. If you're willing, share your relationship goal(s) with the rest of the group.

1.

2.

3.

What connections do you see between these goals
and what you believe to be God's purposes for your
life?

CLOSING PRAYER

*Father, we pray that, for every person in this group,
today will be the start of better understanding what
You want from us and how our relationships can
help us achieve those goals. You have been so loving
and good to us. We just want to respond by doing*

what pleases You. We commit ourselves to that now and throughout the rest of this relationship goals study.

In the name of Jesus, amen.

PREVIEW OF SESSION 2

Next time, we'll be looking at our relationship with God and how putting that relationship first helps all our other relationships fall into line, including our dating relationships. The topic of session 2 is the basis of doing relationship goals differently—don't miss it!

RELATIONSHIP GOALS
SPIRITUALITY

Based on chapters 2 and 3 of *Relationship Goals:* "Before the Person" and "The S-Word."

Session Aim: To show that our relationship with God always comes first, that He made us for relationship, and that as we date others, we should look for someone who will help move us toward God's purposes for us.

No matter what other relationships we have (or don't have), all of us can have a relationship with God. Through Christ, He invites us into the same kind of connection He has within the Trinity—a loving, giving relationship. Even though the top relationship goal we have on our minds right now probably is finding or improving a human relationship, it's important to see how our relationship with God should come first and above all other relationships. It's *the* relationship, and all blessings flow out of that relationship. In fact, one of those blessings is that He enables us to do our other relationships at their highest possible level. When we put God first, He'll bless the rest.

May I make it very plain for you? You can't have the best kind of relationships—you can't win at relationships—without God. Whether it's a friendship, a sibling relationship, a romantic relationship, or whatever it is, it can be pretty good in its own way, and you can come up with great Instagram posts. But when you cut that thing wide open, there are two people who need a Savior. You might have an emotional connection or an intellectual connection or just a strong physical connection, but without God that connection isn't enough.

> *Through Christ, He invites us into the same kind of connection He has within the Trinity—a loving, giving relationship.*

I particularly want to make this point for single people, because single people often feel like they're missing out on relationship or that they're in a waiting period until they can really start living. That is so far from the truth!

If you have single people in your Relationship Goals group, I want to encourage them with this: your singleness may actually be the most important part of the relationship process. It's not a curse. It's an opportunity! It's the best chance you'll ever have to work on being uniquely you—original and distinct. A good period of singleness means learning to be a whole, unique self. God wants you to enjoy this season of life in which you can become whole and complete on your own, apart from a spouse or partner.

Whatever your relationship status, this session is for you because it demonstrates that you should always be working on yourself. Self-work is beneficial in all kinds of relationships. For example, the more you understand about yourself, the easier it is to have mature relationships with your parents or siblings. The more comfortable you are with you, the more people will be attracted to your authenticity and confidence. The more secure you are about your gifts, talents, and calling, the less you'll feel you have to prove.

In the previous session, we saw that if we want to have successful relationships, we need to set goals that are aligned with God's teaching and His purposes for us. In this session, we're going to go way, way back to the beginning of time to find out where relationships come from and what the basics of having relationships are. Sis and bro—this is where we start to build new relational lives.

OPENING PRAYER

Father God, we want to start out our time together today thanking You for creating us out of Your love for us and for sending Your Son so that we can be in relationship with You.

We take You for granted too often. We think the

*problems and people in our lives are more important
than our relationship with You. Help us today to
get a clearer picture of what our relational priorities
should be. Be the Lord of our relationships.*

In Jesus's name, amen.

STARTER QUESTION

What are some of the things you like best about you? (No
jacked-up pride or false humility, please. Say it straight.)

STEP 1: PERSONAL NEED

Sometimes we compartmentalize our faith. We wall it off
from other parts of our life, including our relationships.
The author has done that at times. How about you?

Consider these questions as possible indicators of whether
your relationship with God has spread its influence into
your other relationships:

- Do the people you work with know you are a Christian? How about your neighbors?
- Is your speech any different when you're at church than when you're at other places?

- Have you made any attempts to share about Jesus with any of the unbelievers in your family?
- If you're dating or engaged, where do biblical values play into your relationship?
- Have you ever felt persecuted, or at least dissed, for your faith?
- Do you practice forgiveness when others hurt you? Do you confess and apologize when you've been wrong?
- Do you have a testimony that you're ready to give, as Revelation 12:11 says?
- Do people come to you for prayer or for advice on spiritual and moral issues?

If you're aware of any ways you've separated your faith and your relationships, admit it to the group.

STEP 2: GROUP DISCUSSION

1. No matter what other relationships we have (or don't have), all of us can have a relationship with God. What difference does it make in how you think about relationships to realize that the whole idea of relationship comes from God?

2. Michael says, "You can't have the best kind of relationships—you can't win at relationships—without God." Give an example of a relationship in your life (or the life of someone you know) that proves this to be true.

3. The story of our origins establishes who we are as relational beings. There are some basic principles here that don't change, no matter what new morality is invented or what new #RelationshipGoals image just got a million likes on social media. Check out Genesis 1:26–28:

> God said, "Let us make human beings in our image, to be like us. They will reign over the fish in the sea, the birds in the sky, the livestock, all the wild animals on the earth, and the small animals that scurry along the ground."
>
> So God created human beings in his own image.
> In the image of God he created them;
> male and female he created them.
>
> Then God blessed them and said, "Be fruitful and multiply. Fill the earth and gov-

ern it. Reign over the fish in the sea, the birds in the sky, and all the animals that scurry along the ground."

a. We're made in the image of God and are the kings and queens of the world. What do you think this says about our purpose?

Also, look at Genesis 2:7, 15, 18–25:

The LORD God formed the man from the dust of the ground. He breathed the breath of life into the man's nostrils, and the man became a living person. . . .

The LORD God placed the man in the Garden of Eden to tend and watch over it. . . .

The LORD God said, "It is not good for the man to be alone. I will make a helper who is just right for him." So the LORD God formed from the ground all the wild animals and all the birds of the sky. He brought them to the man to see what he would call them, and the man chose a name for each one. He gave names to all the livestock, all the birds of the sky, and all the wild animals.

But still there was no helper just right
for him.

So the LORD God caused the man to
fall into a deep sleep. While the man slept,
the LORD God took out one of the man's
ribs and closed up the opening. Then the
LORD God made a woman from the rib,
and he brought her to the man.

"At last!" the man exclaimed.

> "This one is bone from my bone,
>   and flesh from my flesh!
> She will be called 'woman,'
>   because she was taken from 'man.'"

This explains why a man leaves his father
and mother and is joined to his wife, and the
two are united into one.

Now the man and his wife were both
naked, but they felt no shame.

b. What do we learn about purpose from this
    passage?

c. What do we learn about relationships?

d. What do we learn about marriage?

4. Do you believe that a major part of God's plan for you involves relationships with others? If so, in what way?

5. Almost all of us have experienced wounds in relationships. How do those wounds point us back to God?

6. Consider your closest friendships. Do they help you become a better person? Draw closer to God? If not, why are you still in them?

7. Do you believe that looking for a relationship that will help you fulfill your God-given purpose is selfish or generous? Why?

8. What couple in your life have you seen thrive because they found their purpose as individuals before they found each other?

Don't allow the pain from your past relationships to make you forfeit your future ones.

9. It takes a lifetime to grow into our God-given purpose. But as you look back on your childhood, what clues can you see about who God created you to be and what gifts He gave you?

10. In what uncomfortable ways is God training you for your purpose?

11. Who in your life has helped push you toward your purpose?

12. What would embracing your current relational season look like on a practical level this week?

13. In what specific ways do you need healing from past relationships before you can move forward into healthier relationships? What is one thing you could do to move toward that healing?

14. If you are single, what are a few ways you can fulfill God's purposes for you that you couldn't if you were married?

15. Michael writes, "You are worth discovering." Do you believe this? Why or why not? What are three specific ways you could grow in your self-awareness?

16. When do you feel most yourself? What are you doing? Whom are you with (if anyone)?

17. Michael says, "Sync up with God's sequence: love God and build relationship with Him, love yourself and embrace your singleness, and then love others." Do you agree with the idea that you have to love yourself in order to love others? Why or why not?

18. Michael writes that singleness is a time to "invest, imagine, and inspire. *Invest* in what you want to see grow in your life. *Imagine* what you could be tomorrow if you started today. And *inspire* others by using everything you have now to make a difference." What specific things could you be doing in this season of life to invest, imagine, and inspire?

STEP 3: ACTION STEP

Maybe this discussion about putting your relationship with God first has made you question whether you even have a relationship with Him at all. If you're not sure you're a believer and follower of Jesus, you *can* be sure. Here's how: "If you openly declare that Jesus is Lord and believe in your heart that God raised him from the dead, you will be saved" (Romans 10:9). Let your Relationship Goals group share in the excitement of your becoming a true follower of Jesus.

> *Most of us spend so much time hating things about ourselves that we don't realize we're crippling our ability to love others.*

Or maybe you are sure you are a believer—in fact, maybe you've been a believer for a long time—but this session has made you realize that other things have begun to crowd out your relationship with God. Maybe today is the time when you need to recommit to making God your number one priority. Share your decision with the group.

And then think through your devotional life. How well are you cultivating your relationship with God?

- How are you doing in Scripture reading and study? (The Bible is the original relationship goals manual, you know.)

- How about spending time with God's people, encouraging them and learning from them? Going to worship services? Taking part in a small group?
- And then, how about prayer? It's simply talking to God. Do you have a prayer habit that works for you?
- What else? What works for you to deepen your relationship with God in this season of your life?

In *Relationship Goals*, Michael says, "Your season of life may have to dictate how you go about pursuing God, but as long as you do it, it's going to be so beneficial, the basis for winning in other areas of your life. I'm convinced God has to be the center of your life." Make sure that He is.

CLOSING PRAYER

God, You're the Relationship Giver. We thank You that we can look forward to an eternity of relationship with You. Help us to make the most of that relationship right now. And continue to teach us how to have better relationships with the people You bring into our lives.

In Jesus's name, amen.

PREVIEW OF SESSION 3

Dating is a fun season of life. But it's not supposed to be just about fun. In session 3, we look at how to turn dating into a tool for preserving and pursuing our mission in life.

RELATIONSHIP GOALS
INTENTIONALITY

Based on chapters 4 and 5 of *Relationship Goals:* "Intentional Dating" and "Does It Need to End?"

Session Aim: To become more intentional about our key relationships, making decisions about beginning them, maintaining them, or ending them based on whether they fulfill our God-given purposes in life and are pleasing to Him.

So many of our relationships are haphazard. We go into them without much thinking—or at least with shallow thinking. We may get lucky with them, but then again, we may not. Too often we see warning signs but we ignore them. Too often we let relationships drag on after they've outlived any real purpose they might have had.

Take dating. Most single people I know are doing what I call recreational dating. Recreational dating is dating that's focused on having fun and getting experiences. It usually means going out with a bunch of different people just because they look good and know how to have a good time. It's usually more about partying than pursuing, more about touching than talking. Recreational dating is the opposite of aiming at a goal; it's like shooting at everything.

> *Dating is not supposed to be a destination. It's supposed to be transportation to where you really want to go.*

This kind of unplanned, careless dating that's focused on short-term enjoyment instead of long-term progress is usually a distraction from your number one relationship—your relationship with God. It can get you into real trouble and can keep you from the good things that relationship ought to bring.

Whether it's dating or any other influential relationship, the point is to be intentional. *Is this relationship moving me toward God or away from Him?* That's the question to ask. You may not be able to choose all your relationships (your mom is your mom). But some you can. Others you can try to upgrade.

Date to try to find a wife or husband who will love you and encourage you to grow in Christ. Take a job working for somebody who has the same standards of honesty and integrity in business that you do. Choose bros or sisters to hang with who use the kinds of words and do the kinds of things that you don't have to feel guilty about. "Whatever you do, do it all for the glory of God" (1 Corinthians 10:31).

I'm not exaggerating when I say that being intentional is the heart of making and pursuing relationship goals.

OPENING PRAYER

Father God, we confess that we are sometimes drawn to relationships that draw us away from You. As we meet together, help us learn to be intentional with our relationships and to trust that Your plan for our lives is better than anything we could ever draw up.

You want us to win in relationship. Today we submit our lives to You, and we will listen and obey.

In Jesus's name, amen.

STARTER QUESTION

What was the worst date you ever went on? Describe it.

STEP 1: PERSONAL NEED

Use the space below to make a list of the most influential people in your life. They might include the following:

- girlfriend or boyfriend, ex-girlfriend or ex-boyfriend if you're still in touch with her or him
- family (parents, siblings, kids, in-laws, extended)
- friends (from work, church, club, neighborhood, school, rooming situation)
- work (bosses, employees, colleagues, clients)
- spiritual leaders

Do *not* include your husband or wife on the list if you are married.

Go back through the list, and put a mark by any names where the relationship is not healthy or positive for you or at least where you think it might be doing more harm than good.

- What makes you concerned about these relationships you've marked?

- What harm has been caused by them?

STEP 2: GROUP DISCUSSION

1. Chapter 4 says, "Recreational dating is like, *I'll date him, then I'll date him, then I'll date him* (or *her, her, her*). It's one-night stands, impulsive infatuations, short-term relationships, and overlapping love affairs, usually with plenty of drama and complications. It's focused pretty much all on the present, with little thought about the future." Have

you dated like that? If you feel comfortable, share about it.

2. What are the costs of recreational dating that you've seen in your own life or the lives of others?

3. Are you currently dating somebody? How long have you been with this person? Do you feel that it's going somewhere or that it's just kind of stuck?

{ *Is this relationship going to push me toward what God has for me, or is it keeping me from that?* }

4. What other kinds of relationships have you gotten into carelessly, without being intentional, and they got you into trouble?

5. Michael says that instead of doing recreational dating, we should do intentional dating. "You might call it dating with purpose. It's dating with the end in mind, wanting to do what pleases the Lord." He goes on to say, "Be selective about whom you're dating, and while you're having fun, also be evaluating what's going on so that you can either bring a misguided relationship to an end before it gets too costly or move it toward a goal if it seems right." What do you think about this idea that the main goal of dating is to figure out whether the other person is a suitable mate? Do you agree or disagree? Why?

6. How would you go about deciding whether someone you're dating really knows and loves the Lord?

7. How would you go about deciding whether the
   person you're dating is somebody who would
   help you move toward God's purposes for your
   life?

8. Besides dating, what are some other kinds of relationships where you think we need to be intentional
   and reflective, rather than casual and careless, in
   whom we choose to be with?

{ *When we don't wait on the Lord,
we give the Enemy the chance to
introduce us to counterfeits.* }

9. Read the following verses, and identify qualities
of people that would make us want to separate
from them.

> I do not spend time with liars
>> or go along with hypocrites.
> I hate the gatherings of those who do evil,
>> and I refuse to join in with the wicked.
>>> (Psalm 26:4–5)

> Stay away from fools,
>> for you won't find knowledge on their lips.
>>> (Proverbs 14:7)

> Don't befriend angry people
>> or associate with hot-tempered people,
> or you will learn to be like them
>> and endanger your soul.
>>> (Proverbs 22:24–25)

> When I wrote to you before, I told you not to
> associate with people who indulge in sexual
> sin. But I wasn't talking about unbelievers
> who indulge in sexual sin, or are greedy, or
> cheat people, or worship idols. You would
> have to leave this world to avoid people like
> that. I meant that you are not to associate
> with anyone who claims to be a believer
> yet indulges in sexual sin, or is greedy, or

worships idols, or is abusive, or is a drunk-
ard, or cheats people. Don't even eat with
such people. (1 Corinthians 5:9–11)

If there is no resurrection, "Let's feast and
drink, for tomorrow we die!" Don't be fooled
by those who say such things, for "bad com-
pany corrupts good character." (1 Corinthians
15:32–33)

a. What relationship killers did you spot in these
passages?

b. How have you experienced these in your
relationships before?

10. A Christian dating a non-Christian is an example
of being unequally yoked—two people pulling
in different directions spiritually. Have you ever
dated an unbeliever, or have you observed a dating

relationship between a believer and a nonbeliever? Describe it. What problems did the spiritual mismatch cause?

11. Michael says dating is supposed to be a temporary passage in life, not a destination. Have you ever kept dating somebody longer than you should have? How did you get into that situation, and how did it affect you and the relationship?

12. Have you ever broken up with somebody you were dating because you realized that person wasn't good for you? Or have you stopped hanging out with a friend or ended some other kind of close relationship for the same reason? What was that like?

13. Get out your Bible and review the story of Abraham, Sarah, Hagar, and Abraham's two sons.

- Act I: God promises a son | Genesis 15:1–16
- Act II: Sarah comes up with a plan to "help" God, and Ishmael is born | Genesis 16
- Act III: God promises a son a second time | Genesis 17:15–22
- Act IV: God promises a son a third time | Genesis 18:1–15
- Act V: Isaac is born, and Hagar and Ishmael are sent away | Genesis 21:1–21

a. What does this story teach us about trusting God for our relationships?

b. What does it teach us about the kinds of things that can go wrong when we don't do relationships God's way?

c. What does it teach us about how God can bring some good out of our relationship mistakes?

d. What does this story remind you of most in your own life?

STEP 3: ACTION STEP

Look back over the list of important relationships you created in step 1. Decide on one or more practical, specific changes you're going to make in your relational life to help you become more like the person you believe God wants you to be. Write them down. Examples:

- If you're single and you've never really thought about your standards for dating and marriage, you could take some time to pray and clarify in your own mind what a potential mate looks like for you. Write down your standards.

- If you've been in a longtime dating relationship and you think the other person is marriage material for you, then you might decide to have a talk about taking it to the next step—engagement.

- If you've been dating and it has become too sexual, you could insist on setting some boundaries.
- If your friend gossips and swears and his example gets you doing the same when you're with him, then have a conversation with him about how you want to have more positive conversations.
- If you have been dating someone who is not a believer or just isn't the kind of person that can help you move toward God, you should break it off. You could do the same for a friendship, business partnership, or other relationship that is unhelpful.

Discuss your plans with someone who can pray for you and keep you accountable. Do the same for that person.

You can do this! And you'll be glad afterward that you did. Remember, "God is working in you, giving you the desire and the power to do what pleases him" (Philippians 2:13).

CLOSING PRAYER

We thank You, Father God, that You are searching our hearts and illuminating our relationships. If anyone in our lives is slowing us down and keeping us from our promise or just picking on our promise, reveal it to us.

God, we need Your help because our hearts are involved. We've made relationships and done things and have been around people for so long that we might not even know how to begin to make relational changes. But Your Word says that You are a good Father, and if we need help for anything, we can ask. So, we ask You to help us move in healthy relationships and right community, with people who are for us and not against us, just as they are for You and not against You.

In Jesus's name, amen.

PREVIEW OF SESSION 4

Is it possible that our culture makes too big a deal of sex—*and* too little? Sex is so powerful that God has designed a specific container for it. If we play around with sex outside that container, we wind up with connections to other people that can hold us back in our purpose for life.

Session 4

RELATIONSHIP GOALS
INTIMACY

Based on chapters 6 and 7 of *Relationship Goals:* "Surrender Your Sexuality" and "All Tied Up."

Session Aim: To learn God's plan for human intimacy, recover from the pain and entanglements of our past sexual mistakes, and honor sex as a gift of God for married couples.

SPECIAL ALERT FROM MIKE!

After writing this book and having countless HOT (Humble, Open, and Transparent) conversations with people, I strongly believe that this session would be more effective and intentional if discussed in same-gender groups. Your group must be a safe space for the purposes of growth and mutual edification and never shame based or a chance to boast about past conquests.

So, it's easy: All my ladies, now let's get in formation and head to another space to chat. And all my fellas, head to the man cave so we can get real.

Relationships are powerful things. The closer the relationship, the more powerful it is. Intimacy can do great good, and it can do great harm.

Sex is the obvious example. Outside the God-ordained sex container—marriage—sex hurts people all the time. Broken hearts. Divorce. Single-parent homes. Disease. Abuse. Inability to trust. Anxiety. Self-loathing. Isolation. Numbness. Coldness to God.

Inside marriage, sex brings a husband and wife back to each other again and again in the most vulnerable and private way. It restores and strengthens their unity. It creates the next generation.

> *The Enemy wants you to think sex has to be sneaky and transgressive, but the truth is . . . sex is good! It's a gift from God to us.*

Other kinds of close relationships are powerful as well. A loving parent-child relationship can launch a healthy, well-rounded, Jesus-loving adult into the world. Two good friends can provide companionship, give perspective, and help each other out when they're facing problems.

We need to surrender our sexual and other relationships to the Lord. Having the same kinds of shallow, selfish, immoral relationship goals that we find in the world means buying counterfeits. God wants us to have the real thing! Our relationship goals aren't worth anything unless they come out of a submitted relationship with God.

So, we need to pay attention to the bonds we are creating with others and make sure they are honoring to God. We want relational bonds that help us in our life journey, not get in our way or detour us where we don't belong.

OPENING PRAYER

Father God, today we pray Romans 12:1–2 for ourselves.

We want to give our bodies to You as a living and holy sacrifice, and we ask that You will find this an acceptable offering. To do this, we ask You to transform the way we think about intimacy so that we will no longer copy the behavior and customs of this world when it comes to intimate relationships.

You have a good, pleasing, and perfect will for each of us. Free us from harmful soul ties and strengthen our helpful soul ties so that we may walk in Your will.

In Jesus's name, amen.

STARTER QUESTION

Who was the first person you had a crush on? When was that? What was that person like?

STEP 1: PERSONAL NEED

It's unbelievable how much something that God meant for good—sex—can be perverted and misused and turned into harm. But it's true. Many of us have gone wrong or have been hurt by others in our sexuality.

Think about any sexual wounding you've received or caused in your lifetime. You may wish to share some of this with your group, but again . . . be wise.

- How are these sexual issues in your life affecting your self-image? Your relationship with God? Your family life and friendships? Your work life? Your goals?

- What do you feel you need to figure out or choose to do differently to get the sexual part of your life right with God?

STEP 2: GROUP DISCUSSION

1. How did you learn about sex? How was that a positive or negative experience for you?

2. Did you grow up thinking sex was a beautiful gift from God or a dirty, secretive thing? Where did those ideas come from?

3. What is your reaction to the idea that sex is supposed to take place only inside marriage?

   ❏ That's a weird and unrealistic idea in this day and age.
   ❏ Of course! It's beautiful.
   ❏ It's biblical . . . but hard to live up to.
   ❏ Other: _____.

4. Surveys show that people who identify as Christians are almost as likely to have sex outside marriage as people who don't identify as Christians. Why do

you think we Christians, as a group, aren't more committed to the idea of marriage being the only sex container in our lives?

5. What excuses have you used (or have you heard other Christians use) to justify sex outside marriage?

{ *What's sometimes called "sexual freedom" isn't free at all. It's actually slavery to sex.* }

6. Our culture tells us that keeping sex in marriage is too restrictive. In what ways is it actually freeing? In what ways is the world's idea of sexual freedom actually slavery to sex?

7. What harm have you seen unbiblical forms of sexual activity cause in people's lives?

8. The apostle Paul wrote about sexual immorality in two letters.

   Look at 1 Corinthians 6:12–20:

   > You say, "I am allowed to do anything"— but not everything is good for you. And even though "I am allowed to do anything," I must not become a slave to anything. You say, "Food was made for the stomach, and the stomach for food." (This is true, though someday God will do away with both of them.) But you can't say that our bodies were made for sexual immorality. They were made for the Lord, and the Lord cares about our bodies. And God will raise us from the dead by his power, just as he raised our Lord from the dead.
   >
   > Don't you realize that your bodies are actually parts of Christ? Should a man take his body, which is part of Christ, and join it to

a prostitute? Never! And don't you realize that if a man joins himself to a prostitute, he becomes one body with her? For the Scriptures say, "The two are united into one." But the person who is joined to the Lord is one spirit with him.

Run from sexual sin! No other sin so clearly affects the body as this one does. For sexual immorality is a sin against your own body. Don't you realize that your body is the temple of the Holy Spirit, who lives in you and was given to you by God? You do not belong to yourself, for God bought you with a high price. So you must honor God with your body.

Then check out 1 Thessalonians 4:3–8:

God's will is for you to be holy, so stay away from all sexual sin. Then each of you will control his own body and live in holiness and honor—not in lustful passion like the pagans who do not know God and his ways. Never harm or cheat a fellow believer in this matter by violating his wife, for the Lord avenges all such sins, as we have solemnly warned you before. God has called us to live holy lives, not impure lives. Therefore, anyone who refuses to

live by these rules is not disobeying human
teaching but is rejecting God, who gives his
Holy Spirit to you.

a. What dos and don'ts about sex do you find in
   these passages?

b. What underlying principles do you see in
   them?

9. Setting aside romantic relationships, have you ever
   had any other close relationships that turned out to
   be unhealthy, unethical, or otherwise dishonoring
   to God? Describe one of these relationships and
   how it affected you.

10. Michael says that all kinds of close relationships form lingering, if not lasting, bonds called soul ties. These ties can be positive or negative or some of both. Name two negative soul ties in your life. Name two positive soul ties.

11. Chapter 7 says, "Every time you have sex with somebody, you are not just joining physically through that action; you are joining emotionally through the intimacy created, and you are joining spiritually because you are two people each with a spiritual nature inside you. So, this is why I say that every time you have sex, you're 'marrying' somebody, just without the covenant." What's your reaction to the idea that a sexual relationship with a boyfriend or girlfriend or hookup is marriage without the covenant?

12. How have soul ties with past romantic partners (whether sex was involved or not) affected you after the relationships were over?

13. Michael says, "The next time you get ready to send private pictures to somebody, or the next time you get ready to slide into the DMs or lie in the bed of somebody who's not your husband or wife, I want you to realize that *you cannot separate sex and Savior.* Christ will be there." Is this a new way of looking at it for you? What do you think about it?

STEP 3: ACTION STEP

Here is the prayer from Chapter 6. If you haven't already prayed it, are you ready to pray it now?

A Prayer of Sexual Surrender

God, I don't know how to do this on my own, so I'm giving You my sexuality. I have done things, said things, experienced things that I know were outside Your will for me. And today I'm asking You to take ownership. I want to live a life of value that is centered in Your love for me and not my desire for temporary fulfillment.

Reset my priorities to purity. Refocus my thoughts on faithfulness. Renew my mind with Your identity for me. Rebuild my self-worth until I truly believe I'm Your masterpiece. Realign my perspective to see myself and others the way You see us. Restore my broken pieces and make me new.

I give You permission to uproot my damaged areas of rejection, pain, hurt, shame, guilt, and bad examples that negatively shaped my perspective. And I'm asking for You to cultivate in me the fruits of the Spirit from Galatians 5 that will produce love, joy, peace, patience, kindness, goodness, faithfulness, gentleness, and self-control. I surrender my sexuality. I'm Yours.

In Jesus's name, amen.

In addition to praying the prayer, write down practical steps you need to take right now to turn your sexuality over to God. Here are a few ideas:

- Tell someone what is going on. Get HOT and share your struggles with a trusted person who will give you spiritual guidance.
- Ask a mentor or trustworthy friend to monitor your online activity.
- Make your phone and computer passwords available to your spouse or someone who will hold you accountable at all times.
- Break up with your girlfriend because your sexual relationship does not honor God.
- Confess to your spouse that you've been having an emotional affair with someone else and you are cutting it off.
- Get rid of the data plan on your phone if the internet is too tempting for you.

- What change do *you* need to make as a sign of surrender to God? *Will you do it?*

Share your decision with one other member of the group. Perhaps the two of you can agree to get in touch with each other later to hold each other accountable for follow-through on your commitments.

CLOSING PRAYER

We agree with You, Father God, that sex is good.
The world has made it dirty. Help us to hold it high,
like You do, so that we won't demean it by treating
it wrongly.

Our sexuality and truly our whole lives are Yours.
We give them to You now and forever.

In Jesus's name, amen.

PREVIEW OF SESSION 5

Finally, we will look at the lasting soul tie of marriage. This tie is so important that it's the one God uses to help us understand the soul tie between Him and the church.

> *You may not be able to get improper sexual habits under control, but God can get them under control if you allow Him.*

RELATIONSHIP GOALS

COMMITMENT

Based on chapters 8, 9, and the conclusion of *Relationship Goals:* "The Triangle," "Major Keys to Successful Marriage," and "Bull's-Eye."

Session Aim: To see how having God in the middle of our most important relationships, especially marriage, can raise them to a level that exceeds our most ambitious relationship goals.

I used to assume that two people who are each at about 50 percent come together, and in combination they make 100 percent or as close to it as they can get. It even seemed biblical, because, as we've seen more than once, we're told, "A man leaves his father and mother and is joined to his wife, and the two are united into one" (Genesis 2:24). In other words, I thought the marriage equation was ½ + ½ = 1. In my mind, that was why people call their spouses "my other half" and say things like "You complete me."

Jerry Maguire is such a liar.

I've been married for some years now, but I realized early on that my original marriage equation was all wrong. The equation for marriage is really this: $1 + 1 + 1 = 1$.

Are you currently questioning everything you learned in second-grade math class? Let me help you. One whole man plus one whole woman plus God in their midst creates one healthy marriage.

If you're married, it's important for your marriage that you've been working on yourself before and during the relationship progression. Hopefully your spouse has been doing the same. But even more important is the presence of the third partner in the marriage. God's participation in the marriage makes it possible for the husband to fulfill his purposes, for the wife to fulfill her purposes, and for the marriage to fulfill its purposes.

> *God's participation in the marriage makes it possible for the husband, the wife, and the marriage to fulfill their purposes.*

I'm not the first to say it, but it's true: A godly marriage is like a triangle. First, the husband and wife are connected at the bottom of the triangle. From day one of their marriage, a wife and husband are bound together in a holy covenant, a soul tie of an awesome sort. The bond is intended to last for a lifetime, and they will hopefully be strengthening their connection and enjoying the rewards of it for as long as they live. Some major keys can help them achieve success in this.

But there's another part of the triangle. God is at the top, with each of the marriage partners spiritually connected to Him (assuming they're both believers in Jesus). This gives them another way to be connected—through God. And look at this: it's a geometric and spiritual truth that as each partner draws closer to God, each one is also drawing closer to the other. The fact that God is in the middle of that marriage is the key to their getting the relationship win.

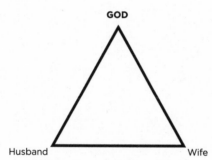

A relationship with God in the middle will always be a whole different kind of animal than a relationship where one or both partners are leaving Him out.

OPENING PRAYER

God, we pray that today each person in this group will get a strong reminder of how important it is

*that You are in the center of our relationships, espe-
cially marriage. Help us to see how You have more
for marriages as couples pursue each other and
pursue You.*

In Jesus's name, amen.

STARTER QUESTION

What would you say is the best marriage you have ever
personally observed? What made it so great, in your view?

STEP 1: PERSONAL NEED

If you are married, complete activity A. If you are not married, complete activity B.

A. Check each box that applies to your marital relationship.

- ❑ We arbelievers in Jesus.
- ❑ We pray together regularly and/or attend
  a small group together.

❑   We go to church together regularly.

❑   When we have a decision to make, we seek God's leading for it.

❑   We discuss what we're reading in Scripture, what we heard in sermons, or what we've learned in Christian books, blogs, or videos.

❑   We both try to serve one another.

❑   Giving to the Lord's work is a central part of our financial planning.

❑   We feel that we have a God-given mission as a couple and are pursuing it together.

Don't take the above quiz *too* seriously. These are just a few possible indicators of spiritual health in a marriage, and there's no one way to go about serving Christ together as a married couple. *But* . . . do take seriously the importance of the active and powerful presence of God in a marriage.

> *With Christ's help, there are practical ways we can get marriages to where they really do reflect the relationship Jesus has with the church.*

If your spouse is in the group, compare your answers to the quiz. Discuss what you think about the ways God is present and active in the marriage.

B. Identify the top three to five most important relationships in your life. Would you say that you are in spiritual agreement with these people? How does that affect the relationships?

STEP 2: GROUP DISCUSSION

1. Overall, what was your impression of the institution of marriage as you were growing up? Why?

2. Michael says, "The real mark of love is giving, and giving takes sacrifice. That's why Ephesians 5:25 says this for husbands: 'Love your wives, just as Christ loved the church. He gave up his life for her.'

And wives are to submit to their husbands (verse 22)." In what ways does a healthy marriage involve sacrifice?

3. What does it mean for God to be the focus of a marriage or dating relationship? What does that look like on a daily, practical level?

4. Chapter 8 states, "When you're in marriage and committed to each other for life, you will discover a fuller, more mature kind of love—one that isn't all caught up in her looks and his sense of humor and having fun and cuddling but realizes just how much you have to give to each other." Do you believe that real love doesn't come until after marriage? Why or why not?

5. Jesus says, "If any of you wants to be my follower, you must give up your own way, take up your cross daily, and follow me" (Luke 9:23). What does dying to yourself mean? How does dying to yourself draw you closer to God?

6. How do you know when someone is thinking, *What can I get out of this relationship? What's in it for me?* in a relationship with you?

7. How does having a covenant with another person affect the relationship?

{
I'm not sure what you're turning from, but I know who you need to turn to. It's Jesus.
}

8. The primary passage on marriage in the New Testament is Ephesians 5:21–33. But if we look closely, we'll realize it's just as much about Christ and the church.

> Submit to one another out of reverence for Christ.
>
> For wives, this means submit to your husbands as to the Lord. For a husband is the head of his wife as Christ is the head of the church. He is the Savior of his body, the church. As the church submits to Christ, so you wives should submit to your husbands in everything.
>
> For husbands, this means love your wives, just as Christ loved the church. He gave up his life for her to make her holy and clean, washed by the cleansing of God's word. He did this to present her to himself as a glorious church without a spot or wrinkle or any other blemish. Instead, she will be holy and without fault. In the same way, husbands ought to love their wives as they love their own bodies. For a man who loves his wife actually shows love for himself. No one hates his own body but feeds and cares for it, just as Christ cares for the church. And we are members of his body.
>
> As the Scriptures say, "A man leaves his

father and mother and is joined to his wife, and the two are united into one." This is a great mystery, but it is an illustration of the way Christ and the church are one. So again I say, each man must love his wife as he loves himself, and the wife must respect her husband.

a. In what ways does this passage compare marriage to the relationship between Christ and His bride, the church?

b. How does this passage help to correct some faulty view of marriage you have had?

9. Michael says, "Even when you're married, you should never stop being 'single.' What I'm talking about here is being an individual and pursuing the godly purposes and goals you have for yourself, personally." If you are married, in what

ways could you work on your singleness as far as pursuing God's vision for your life? In what ways could you help your spouse work on her singleness?

10. How does improving yourself individually add to a marriage?

11. (For women) In chapter 9, Natalie Todd lists three things women need from their husbands: security, affection, and communication. Which of the "women need" statements do you think men most need to hear, and why?

12. (For men) In chapter 9, Natalie Todd lists some things that men need from their wives: honor

and respect, support, and sex. Which of the "men need" statements do you think women most need to hear, and why?

13. If a couple have developed poor habits of communication, what are some good ways to change to good habits?

14. Gary Chapman has identified five love languages: physical touch, quality time, words of affirmation, acts of service, and gifts. If you have taken one of Chapman's love language quizzes or you just want to guess, what are your top two languages? What are your bf's/gf's or spouse's top two love languages?

15. From your experience, what are the differences be-
    tween good fighting and bad fighting in a marriage?

16. Do you have any final comments or advice about
    marriage you're dying to share with the group? Do
    so now.

STEP 3: ACTION STEP

If you are married, choose step A. If you are not married,
choose step B.

A. Have a talk with your husband or wife about the
spiritual side of your marriage. Use the acronym ONE that
Michael describes in chapter 8 of *Relationship Goals*.

O—*Ownership*. Before God in prayer, commit together that you will take ownership of your own responsibilities in the marriage and look to Him as the
   owner of the relationship. Make this a turning point

in your relationship—one that you can look back on as the time when you clearly and openly committed together to follow God as a couple.

N—*Nurture*. Discuss how you, as a couple, can improve your devotion to God, such as in your praying, worshipping, serving, and giving. Discuss also how you would like to be nurtured by each other. Make a plan. Write down the things you agree on in this conversation.

E—*Evolve*. Discuss the future. How do you see your marriage strengthening and changing over time? How do you think God might be calling you to serve Him as a couple? What preparations might that service require you to start on now?

B. Avoiding being unequally yoked—partnered too closely with unbelievers in your key relationships—is one thing. Actually pursuing spiritual unity in relationships is another. Consider what this looks like for you. Maybe you should bring the conversation around to faith more with your best friend. Or have a conversation with a business colleague about how your beliefs and morals will impact your business decisions.

LAST STEP: CONCLUDING GROUP DISCUSSION

17. Michael Todd loves to quote Philippians 2:13: "God is working in you, giving you the desire and the power to do what pleases him." As you look

back over not just this session but the whole *Relationship Goals* study, what are your desires for relationship goals now? How are you seeing God equip you to win at these goals?

18. If the rest of the group were to check up with you in six months, what changes would you hope they would see in your relational life?

CLOSING PRAYER

Father, whether we're single or married, whether we have kids or don't have kids, we acknowledge that Your rightful place is at the head of our household. In all our relationships with other believers, help us preserve unity in the Spirit. In our relationships with unbelievers, enable us to show what it is like to put You first so that they, too, might begin to have relationship goals that revolve around You.

We thank You for the special gift of marriage. For

those in the group who are married, we ask that You will remind them daily that if they draw closer to You, they will also draw closer to each other. Your Word says, "Let no one split apart what God has joined together," so we pray that no attack of the Enemy will be able to come against any one of these marriages. May every marriage here present a clear picture of Your love for all the world to see.

In Jesus's name, amen.

RELATIONSHIP REFERENCES

Genesis 1:26–28

- genders
- reproduction

God said, "Let us make human beings in our image, to be like us. They will reign over the fish in the sea, the birds in the sky, the livestock, all the wild animals on the earth, and the small animals that scurry along the ground."

So God created human beings in his own image.
In the image of God he created them;
male and female he created them.

Then God blessed them and said, "Be fruitful and multiply. Fill the earth and govern it. Reign over the fish in the sea, the birds in the sky, and all the animals that scurry along the ground."

Genesis 2:18–25

- marriage
- marital sex

The LORD God said, "It is not good for the man to be alone. I will make a helper who is just right for him." So the LORD God formed from the ground all the wild animals and all the birds of the sky. He brought them to the man to see what he would call them, and the man chose a name for each one. He gave names to all the livestock, all the birds of the sky, and all the wild animals. But still there was no helper just right for him.

So the LORD God caused the man to fall into a deep sleep. While the man slept, the LORD God took out one of the man's ribs and closed up the opening. Then the LORD God made a woman from the rib, and he brought her to the man.

"At last!" the man exclaimed.

> "This one is bone from my bone,
>   and flesh from my flesh!
> She will be called 'woman,'
>   because she was taken from 'man.'"

This explains why a man leaves his father and mother and is joined to his wife, and the two are united into one.

Now the man and his wife were both naked, but they felt no shame.

Exodus 20:14
(see also Deuteronomy 5:18)

- adultery

You must not commit adultery.

Deuteronomy 24:1–4

- divorce
- remarriage

"Suppose a man marries a woman but she does not please him. Having discovered something wrong with her, he writes a document of divorce, hands it to her, and sends her away from his house. When she leaves his house, she is free to marry another man. But if the second husband also turns against her, writes a document of divorce, hands it to her, and sends her away, or if he dies, the first husband may not marry her again, for she has been defiled. That would be detestable to the LORD. You must not bring guilt upon the land the LORD your God is giving you as a special possession."

Malachi 2:13–16

- adultery
- divorce
- marriage
- reproduction

Here is another thing you do. You cover the LORD's altar with tears, weeping and groaning because he pays no attention to your offerings and doesn't accept them with pleasure. You cry out, "Why doesn't the LORD accept my worship?" I'll tell you why! Because the LORD witnessed the vows you and your wife made when you were young. But you have been unfaithful to her, though she remained your faithful partner, the wife of your marriage vows.

Didn't the LORD make you one with your wife? In body and spirit you are his. And what does he want? Godly children from your union. So guard your heart; remain loyal to the wife of your youth. "For I hate divorce!" says the LORD, the God of Israel. "To divorce your wife is to overwhelm her with cruelty," says the LORD of Heaven's Armies. "So guard your heart; do not be unfaithful to your wife."

Matthew 5:27–30

- adultery
- lust

"You have heard the commandment that says, 'You must not commit adultery.' But I say, anyone who even looks at a woman with lust has already committed adultery with her in his heart. So if your eye—even your good eye—causes you to lust, gouge it out and throw it away. It is better for you to lose one part of your body than for your whole body to be thrown into hell. And if your hand—even your stronger hand—causes you to sin, cut it off and throw it away. It is better for you to lose one part of your body than for your whole body to be thrown into hell."

Matthew 5:31–32 (see also Luke 16:18)

- adultery
- divorce
- remarriage

"You have heard the law that says, 'A man can divorce his wife by merely giving her a written notice of divorce.' But I say that a man who divorces his wife, unless she has been unfaithful, causes her to commit adultery. And anyone who marries a divorced woman also commits adultery."

Matthew 19:3–12 (see also Mark 10:2–12)

- divorce
- marriage
- remarriage
- adultery
- celibacy

Some Pharisees came and tried to trap [Jesus] with this question: "Should a man be allowed to divorce his wife for just any reason?"

"Haven't you read the Scriptures?" Jesus replied. "They record that from the beginning 'God made them male and female.'" And he said, "'This explains why a man leaves his father and mother and is joined to his wife, and the two are united into one.' Since they are no longer two but one, let no one split apart what God has joined together."

"Then why did Moses say in the law that a man could give his wife a written notice of divorce and send her away?" they asked.

Jesus replied, "Moses permitted divorce only as a concession to your hard hearts, but it was not what God had originally intended. And I tell you this, whoever divorces his wife and marries someone else commits adultery—unless his wife has been unfaithful."

Jesus' disciples then said to him, "If this is the case, it is better not to marry!"

"Not everyone can accept this statement," Jesus said. "Only those whom God helps. Some are born as eunuchs, some have been made eunuchs by others, and some choose not to marry for the sake of the Kingdom of Heaven. Let anyone accept this who can."

1 Corinthians 6:12–20

- sexual immorality

You say, "I am allowed to do anything"—but not everything is good for you. And even though "I am allowed to do anything," I must not become a slave to anything. You say, "Food was made for the stomach, and the stomach for food." (This is true, though someday God will do away with both of them.) But you can't say that our bodies were made for sexual immorality. They were made for the Lord, and the Lord cares about our bodies. And God will raise us from the dead by his power, just as he raised our Lord from the dead.

Don't you realize that your bodies are actually parts of Christ? Should a man take his body, which is part of Christ, and join it to a prostitute? Never! And don't you realize that if a man joins himself to a prostitute, he becomes one body with her? For the Scriptures say, "The two are united into one." But the person who is joined to the Lord is one spirit with him.

Run from sexual sin! No other sin so clearly affects the body as this one does. For sexual immorality is a sin against your own body. Don't you realize that your body is the temple of the Holy Spirit, who lives in you and was given to you by God? You do not belong to yourself, for God bought you with a high price. So you must honor God with your body.

1 Corinthians 7:1–2

- celibacy
- marriage

Yes, it is good to abstain from sexual relations. But because there is so much sexual immorality, each man should have his own wife, and each woman should have her own husband.

1 Corinthians 7:3–6

- marital sex

The husband should fulfill his wife's sexual needs, and the wife should fulfill her husband's needs. The wife gives authority over her body to her husband, and the husband gives authority over his body to his wife.

Do not deprive each other of sexual relations, unless you both agree to refrain from sexual intimacy for a limited time so you can give yourselves more completely to prayer. Afterward, you should come together again so that Satan won't be able to tempt you because of your lack of self-control. I say this as a concession, not as a command.

1 Corinthians 7:7–9

- singleness
- marriage
- lust

I wish everyone were single, just as I am. Yet each person has a special gift from God, of one kind or another.

So I say to those who aren't married and to widows—it's better to stay unmarried, just as I am. But if they can't control themselves, they should go ahead and marry. It's better to marry than to burn with lust.

1 Corinthians 7:10–11

- divorce
- remarriage

For those who are married, I have a command that comes not from me, but from the Lord. A wife must not leave her husband. But if she does leave him, let her remain single or else be reconciled to him. And the husband must not leave his wife.

1 Corinthians 7:12–16

- divorce
- remarriage

I will speak to the rest of you, though I do not have a direct command from the Lord. If a fellow believer has a wife who is not a believer and she is willing to continue living with him, he must not leave her. And if a believing woman has a husband who is not a believer and he is willing to continue living with her, she must not leave him. For the believing wife brings holiness to her marriage, and the believing husband brings holiness to his marriage. Otherwise, your children would not be holy, but now they are holy. (But if the husband or wife who isn't a believer insists on leaving, let them go. In such cases the believing husband or wife is no longer bound to the other, for God has called you to live in peace.) Don't you wives realize that your husbands might be saved because of you? And don't you husbands realize that your wives might be saved because of you?

1 Corinthians 7:25–38

- singleness
- marriage

Now regarding your question about the young women who are not yet married. I do not have a command from the Lord for them. But the Lord in his mercy has given me wisdom that can be trusted, and I will share it with you. Because of the present crisis, I think it is best to remain as you are. If you have a wife, do not seek to end the marriage. If you do not have a wife, do not seek to get married. But if you do get married, it is not a sin. And if a young woman gets married, it is not a sin. However, those who get married at this time will have troubles, and I am trying to spare you those problems.

But let me say this, dear brothers and sisters: The time that remains is very short. So from now on, those with wives should not focus only on their marriage. Those who weep or who rejoice or who buy things should not be absorbed by their weeping or their joy or their possessions. Those who use the things of the world should not become attached to them. For this world as we know it will soon pass away.

I want you to be free from the concerns of this life. An unmarried man can spend his time doing the Lord's work and thinking how to please him. But a married man has to think about his earthly responsibilities and how to please his wife. His interests are divided. In the same way, a woman who is no longer married or has never been married can be devoted to the Lord and holy in body and in spirit. But a married woman has to think about her earthly responsibilities and how to please her husband. I am saying this for your benefit, not to place restrictions on you. I want you to do whatever will help you serve the Lord best, with as few distractions as possible.

But if a man thinks that he's treating his fiancée improperly and will inevitably give in to his passion, let him marry her as he wishes. It is not a sin. But if he has decided firmly not to marry and there is no urgency and he can control his passion, he does well not to marry. So the person who marries his fiancée does well, and the person who doesn't marry does even better.

1 Corinthians 7:39–40

- divorce
- remarriage
- singleness

A wife is bound to her husband as long as he lives. If her husband dies, she is free to marry anyone she wishes, but only if he loves the Lord. But in my opinion it would be better for her to stay single, and I think I am giving you counsel from God's Spirit when I say this.

Ephesians 5:21–33
(see also Colossians 3:18–19)

- marriage

Submit to one another out of reverence for Christ.

For wives, this means submit to your husbands as to the Lord. For a husband is the head of his wife as Christ is the head of the church. He is the Savior of his body, the church. As the church submits to Christ, so you wives should submit to your husbands in everything.

For husbands, this means love your wives, just as Christ loved the church. He gave up his life for her to make her holy and clean, washed by the cleansing of God's word. He did this to present her to himself as a glorious church without a spot or wrinkle or any other blemish. Instead, she will be holy and without fault. In the same way, husbands ought to love their wives as they love their own bodies. For a man who loves his wife actually shows love for himself.

No one hates his own body but feeds and cares for it, just as Christ cares for the church. And we are members of his body.

As the Scriptures say, "A man leaves his father and mother and is joined to his wife, and the two are united into one." This is a great mystery, but it is an illustration of the way Christ and the church are one. So again I say, each man must love his wife as he loves himself, and the wife must respect her husband.

1 Thessalonians 4:3-8

- sexual immorality
- adultery

God's will is for you to be holy, so stay away from all sexual sin. Then each of you will control his own body and live in holiness and honor—not in lustful passion like the pagans who do not know God and his ways. Never harm or cheat a fellow believer in this matter by violating his wife, for the Lord avenges all such sins, as we have solemnly warned you before. God has called us to live holy lives, not impure lives. Therefore, anyone who refuses to live by these rules is not disobeying human teaching but is rejecting God, who gives his Holy Spirit to you.

Hebrews 13:4

- sexual immorality
- adultery

Give honor to marriage, and remain faithful to one another in marriage. God will surely judge people who are immoral and those who commit adultery.

1 Peter 3:1–7

- marriage

In the same way, you wives must accept the authority of your husbands. Then, even if some refuse to obey the Good News, your godly lives will speak to them without any words. They will be won over by observing your pure and reverent lives.

Don't be concerned about the outward beauty of fancy hairstyles, expensive jewelry, or beautiful clothes. You should clothe yourselves instead with the beauty that comes from within, the unfading beauty of a gentle and quiet spirit, which is so precious to God. This is how the holy women of old made themselves beautiful. They put their trust in God and accepted the authority of their husbands. For instance, Sarah obeyed her husband, Abraham, and called him her master. You are her daughters when you do what is right without fear of what your husbands might do.

In the same way, you husbands must give honor to your wives. Treat your wife with understanding as you live together. She may be weaker than you are, but she is your equal partner in God's gift of new life. Treat her as you should so your prayers will not be hindered.

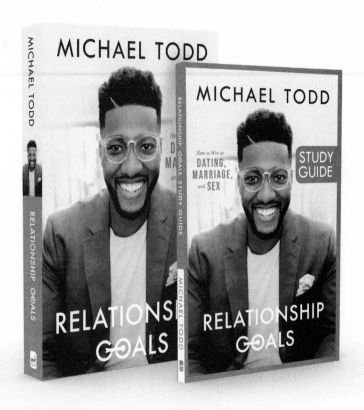

Find helpful resources, videos, downloads and more at IAmMikeTodd.com!